ROBOT

Written by
CLIVE GIFFORD

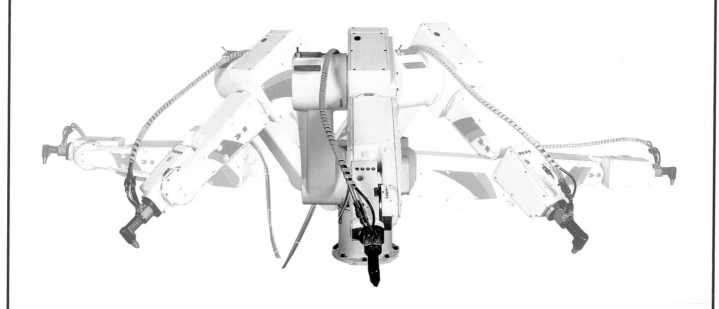

FIREFLY BOOKS

Elma – an intelligent
robot that can teach
itself to walk

A DK PUBLISHING BOOK

Project editor Kitty Blount
Art editor Carlton Hibbert
DTP designers Nicola Studdart, Andrew O'Brien
Senior managing editor Linda Martin
Senior managing art editor Julia Harris
Picture research Angela Anderson
Production Lisa Moss
Jacket design Dean Price

Photography Geoff Brightling
Modelmakers Peter Minister Model FX,
Dave Morgan, Chris Reynolds and the BBC team

First published in Canada in 1998
by Firefly Books Ltd.
3680 Victoria Park Avenue
Willowdale, Ontario, Canada
M2H 3 K1
2 4 6 8 10 9 7 5 3 1

Canadian Cataloguing in Publication Data

Gifford, Clive
Robot

(Inside guides) Includes index.
ISBN 1-55209-276-3

1. Robots – Juvenile literature.
I. Title II. Series

TJ211.2.G53 1998   j629.8'92 C98-931084-1

Reproduced in Italy by
GRB Editrice S.r.l., Verona
Printed in Singapore by Toppan

Robart III – a
security guard robot

Pioneer 1 robot,
adapted to play
robot football

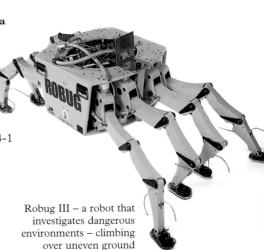

Robug II – a research
robot – scaling a wall

Robug III – a robot that
investigates dangerous
environments – climbing
over uneven ground

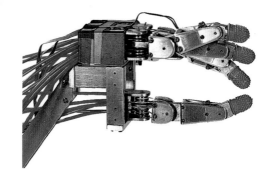

Contents

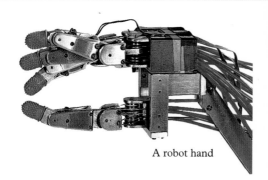

A robot hand

What is a robot? 8

Computer control 10

Arm power 12

In the factory 14

Artificial intelligence 16

AGV systems 18

Difficult terrain 20

Power of vision 22

Performing surgery 24

26 Sheep shearing

28 Exploring space

30 Missions on Mars

32 Working underwater

34 Getting a grip

36 Remote operation

38 Nanorobots

40 Robots in the near future

42 Glossary and index

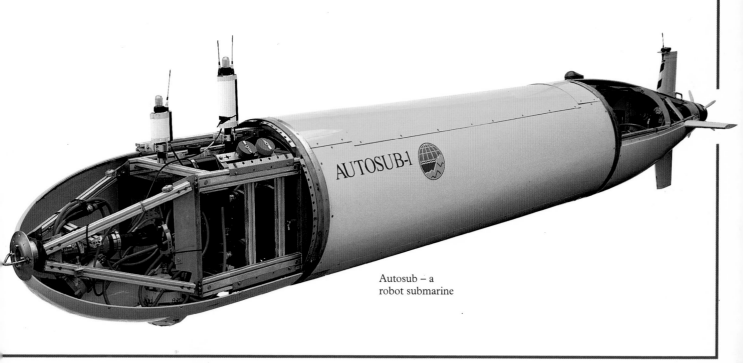

Autosub – a
robot submarine

What is a robot?

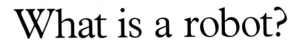

Robots are one of the newest and most exciting types of machines. They can carry out certain tasks by moving in a similar way to humans, but with greater strength and precision. Robots can operate in situations tough or impossible for a human to work in, such as deep underwater, in a fire, or on another planet. They also free humans from having to perform dull, repetitive tasks such as spray-painting cars. Essentially, a robot is an automated machine that performs human-styled actions and reacts to some external events, as well as to prerecorded commands.

Smooth edges
Different end effectors can be attached here depending on the job at hand. This one is for smoothing rough edges in metalwork.

Finding the way
InteleCady uses an array of sensors to avoid bunkers, golfers, and other obstacles.

Automata for the people
Mechanical moving figures, such as this archer doll that can pick up and fire arrows, are known as automata. Automata, however, cannot react to their environment or be reprogrammed easily like robots.

InteleCady controller
The robot has a built-in digital map of the course it works on.

Moving parts
Often it is only a part of a robot that moves. With many mobile robots, such as this, the whole robot can move.

InteleCady
Many robots, like this InteleCady robot golf bag carrier, have sensors, which are devices that provide feedback on the robot's environment and situation, just like a human's senses do.

Robot anatomy
Most robots, including this armored patrol robot from the Robotix 4000 Kit® made by Learning Curve Toys, have certain important parts in common. They have a drive system, a controller, moving parts, and an end effector.

Wired to the controller
Wires from the motors are attached to the controller. The controller is like a small computer that is either remote-controlled by a human operator or preprogrammed.

End effector
A robot part that can manipulate objects or the environment around it is called an end effector. This robot gripper is a common end effector.

Drive
The drive system powers the robot to move itself or some of its parts. This robot's drive system is a number of small, battery-powered electric motors, one of which drives these wheels.

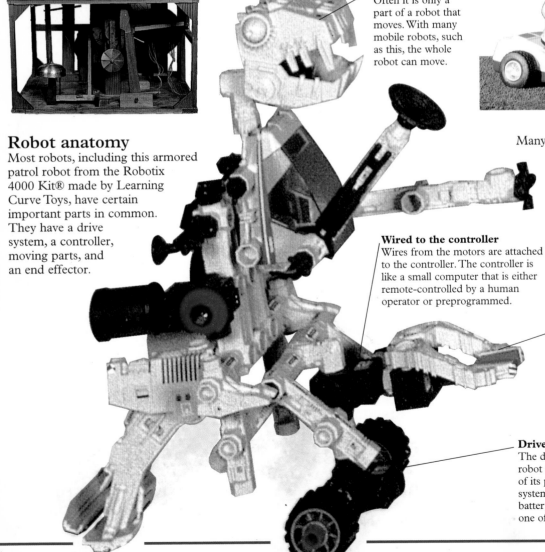

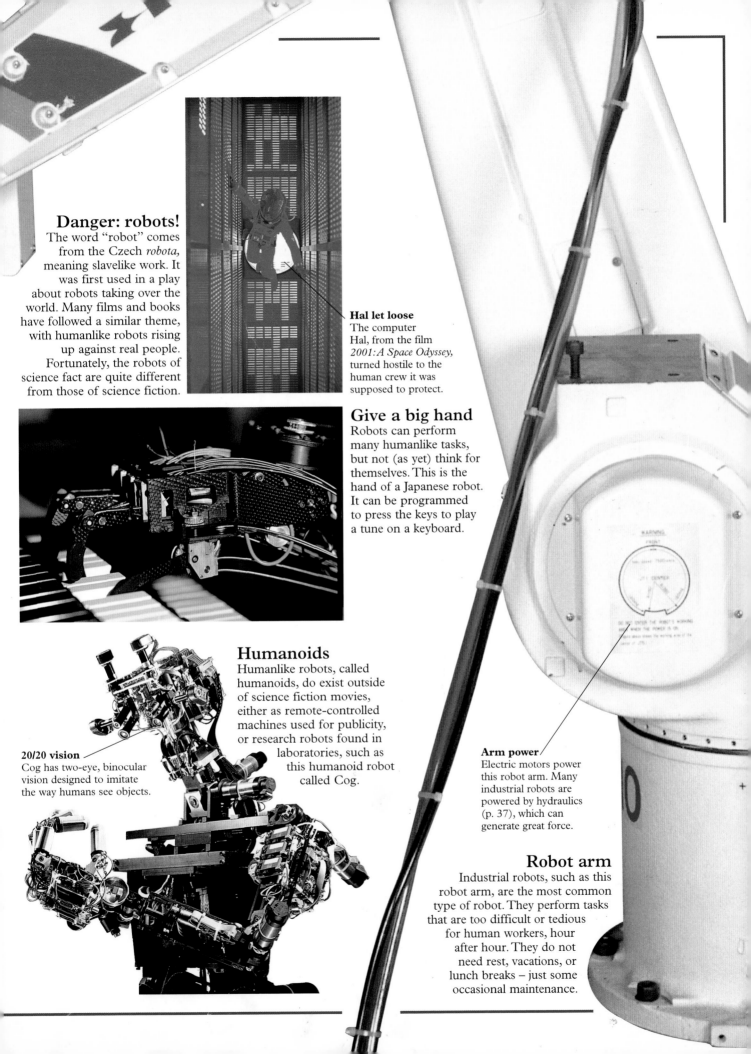

Danger: robots!
The word "robot" comes from the Czech *robota,* meaning slavelike work. It was first used in a play about robots taking over the world. Many films and books have followed a similar theme, with humanlike robots rising up against real people. Fortunately, the robots of science fact are quite different from those of science fiction.

Hal let loose
The computer Hal, from the film *2001: A Space Odyssey,* turned hostile to the human crew it was supposed to protect.

Give a big hand
Robots can perform many humanlike tasks, but not (as yet) think for themselves. This is the hand of a Japanese robot. It can be programmed to press the keys to play a tune on a keyboard.

Humanoids
Humanlike robots, called humanoids, do exist outside of science fiction movies, either as remote-controlled machines used for publicity, or research robots found in laboratories, such as this humanoid robot called Cog.

20/20 vision
Cog has two-eye, binocular vision designed to imitate the way humans see objects.

Arm power
Electric motors power this robot arm. Many industrial robots are powered by hydraulics (p. 37), which can generate great force.

Robot arm
Industrial robots, such as this robot arm, are the most common type of robot. They perform tasks that are too difficult or tedious for human workers, hour after hour. They do not need rest, vacations, or lunch breaks – just some occasional maintenance.

Computer control

Robots need to be told what to do – but not just a command such as "pick up that bolt over there." A robot needs a set of precise instructions telling it how it has to move all of its parts to achieve its objective. Most robots receive these instructions from a computer or microprocessor. Computer programs send electrical signals to the robot's controller or directly to drive system components called actuators, which move the robot's parts. These signals allow the robot to perform its tasks.

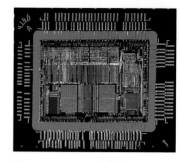

Computer chip
At the heart of a computer lie silicon chips, containing millions of switches. Electrical signals pass information to a computer program indicating whether the switches are "on" or "off." Binary numbers in the program correspond to the signals – one for "on" and zero for "off."

Controller
The electronic devices are housed inside the robot's controller. These convert digital signals from the computer to analog signals that the robot's actuators understand.

Wires carrying signals
Once converted, the signals travel along wires running to each actuator.

Making it move
The actuator is a type of electric motor called a servo that makes individual parts of the robot move.

Firm grip
An ordinary pencil eraser helps give the robot grip as the other legs move.

Test beans
In testing, it is recommended that dried beans are used instead of messy coffee!

Soft touch
There is a glide wheel made of nylon attached to each leg.

Instant automatons
Robots are available in kits for schools and individuals to build and learn from. This three-legged crawler (above), built from the Robix™ RCS–6 construction set, can be programmed to move across a surface in a shuffle, walk, or gallop. It is one of many robots in the same kit, including the catapult and coffeemaker (right).

Coffee break
Making a cup of coffee is an easy task for you, but for a robot it is a complicated series of actions. Just stirring a cup of coffee involves a large number of different computer-controlled processes. The robot must find the cup, insert the spoon, stop moving the spoon down before it hits the bottom, and then stir the liquid around at a set speed.

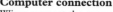

Computer connection
Wires connect the servos to the robot's controller, which is connected by cable to the computer. The cable sends digital signals from the computer to the robot.

Full swing
The end effector moves forward at high speed, throwing the ball.

Computer communication
Robots do not have to be linked by cable to their computer. The controller for the Lego™ Mindstorms robot-making kit uses an infrared link to download programs from a computer.

RCX controller clipped to robot

Balancing the ball
The program instructs the servos to move the end effector slowly back, keeping the ball balanced.

Repeated action
Once the computer program has been tuned for the right distance, the robot is able to repeat its steps, with over 90 percent accuracy.

Catapult
When programmed, a robot can repeat the precise same set of movements with far more accuracy than humans. Try throwing a table tennis ball into a cup a yard away. You will have some success, but not as much as this robot catapult, which gets the ball in almost every time.

Robot construction
Metal links allow different shapes of robot to be constructed.

Work station
The robot must turn and reach around its working area to collect the coffee ingredients and place them correctly.

Operating the robot
Each servo is controlled from a computer program or moved directly by the user from the computer's keyboard.

Coffee scoop
The teaspoon is the robot's end effector. It is held in place by foam blocks.

A different servo powers each joint

Steady base
The robot's base is weighted to stop the arm overbalancing.

Arm power

Although robots come in many shapes and sizes, robot arms are by far the most common. They have been around since the start of robotics. Initially robot arms were built for use in factories. While they are still widely used in industry, robot arms are now often found in research laboratories and installed in mobile robot vehicles also. Often based on the human arm, robot arms usually have shoulder, elbow, and wrist joints. Some even have a waist joint, like the industrial robot below. Robot arms are driven by pneumatic or hydraulic power (p. 37) or electrical motors.

First-ever robot
The very first working robot, called the Unimate, was a robot arm, built in 1961. Used for metal die-casting, the Unimate was a great success. It was first guided through its task in steps, which were recorded. When played back, the robot automatically performed its task.

Electric motor
Electricity produces one magnetic field around the stator coil and an opposing field around the rotor. As the rotor turns to try to align the two magnetic fields, the field around the stator coil is reversed. When this is done constantly, the rotor spins around, driving the shaft.

Shaft connected to gear wheels, which drive part of the robot

Shaft joined to rotor

Stator coils

Rotor

Fast mover
The arm's electric motors move its joints at high speeds, up to 5 ft (1.5 m) per second. This makes it suitable for speedy assembly-line work.

Hard worker
The arm is designed for vigorous use in tough factory environments. It weighs over 330 lbs (150 kg).

Degrees of freedom
Each different plane or direction that a part of the robot can move is called a degree of freedom. This robot arm has six degrees of freedom. It can turn at its waist and move at the shoulder and elbow. Its wrist can move in three different sets of directions. Some robot arms obtain a seventh additional degree of freedom by being placed on sliding rails, allowing the arm to move along too.

Placing the end effector
A robot arm's joints are driven to move so that the end effector is in a position to work.

Different tasks
The arm can be installed with different end effectors for different tasks. This one is for smoothing rough edges in metalwork.

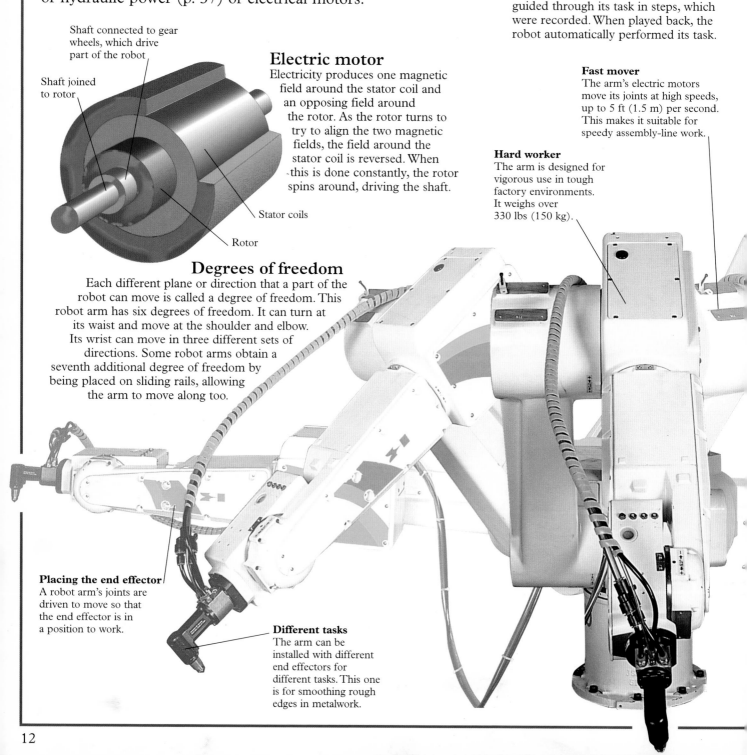

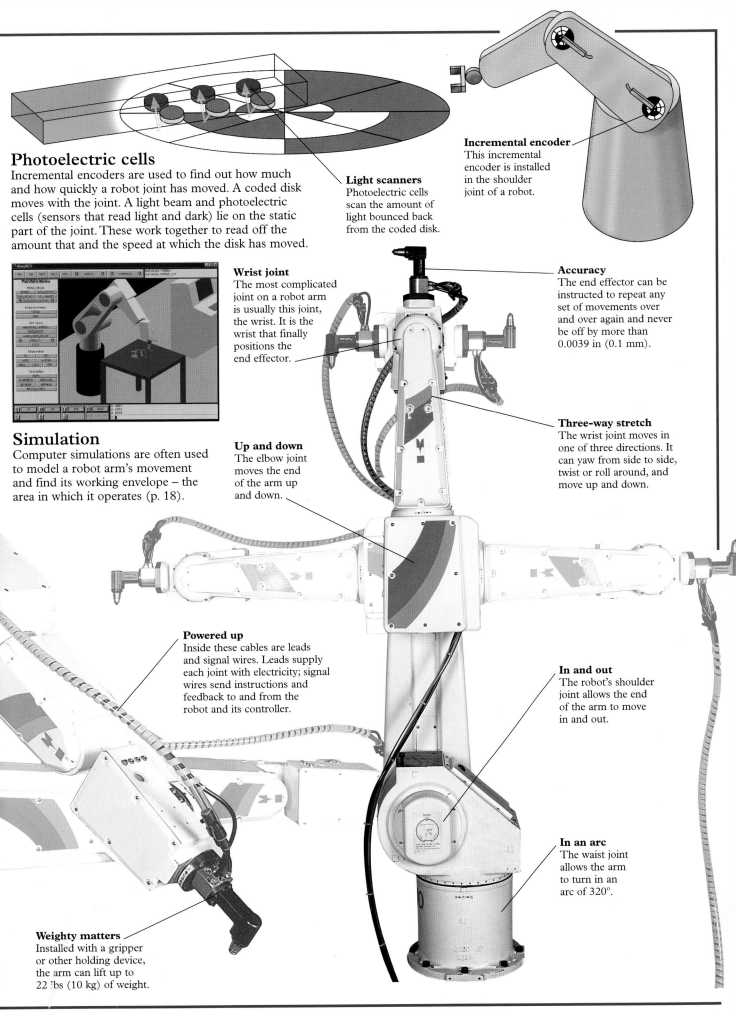

Photoelectric cells

Incremental encoders are used to find out how much and how quickly a robot joint has moved. A coded disk moves with the joint. A light beam and photoelectric cells (sensors that read light and dark) lie on the static part of the joint. These work together to read off the amount that and the speed at which the disk has moved.

Light scanners
Photoelectric cells scan the amount of light bounced back from the coded disk.

Incremental encoder
This incremental encoder is installed in the shoulder joint of a robot.

Wrist joint
The most complicated joint on a robot arm is usually this joint, the wrist. It is the wrist that finally positions the end effector.

Accuracy
The end effector can be instructed to repeat any set of movements over and over again and never be off by more than 0.0039 in (0.1 mm).

Simulation

Computer simulations are often used to model a robot arm's movement and find its working envelope – the area in which it operates (p. 18).

Up and down
The elbow joint moves the end of the arm up and down.

Three-way stretch
The wrist joint moves in one of three directions. It can yaw from side to side, twist or roll around, and move up and down.

Powered up
Inside these cables are leads and signal wires. Leads supply each joint with electricity; signal wires send instructions and feedback to and from the robot and its controller.

In and out
The robot's shoulder joint allows the end of the arm to move in and out.

In an arc
The waist joint allows the arm to turn in an arc of 320°.

Weighty matters
Installed with a gripper or other holding device, the arm can lift up to 22 lbs (10 kg) of weight.

In the factory

Robotics grew largely out of advances in factory machinery, much of which is automated, working without human intervention. Unlike a piece of automated machinery, a robot can be programmed and reprogrammed to perform a chain of different actions. By changing a program, a robot can be made to vary its actions. Today, the majority of robots can be found in factories, doing tough, exacting work that is difficult or unpleasant for human workers. There are over 150,000 industrial robots in factories worldwide, performing such tasks as spray-painting, welding, and packaging.

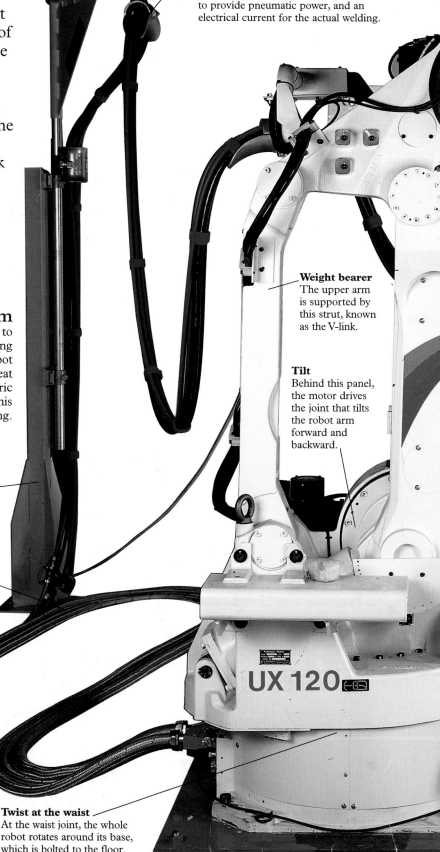

Air, water, and electricity
A collection of cables, which runs all the way to the end effector, includes pipes carrying water for cooling, air used to provide pneumatic power, and an electrical current for the actual welding.

Weight bearer
The upper arm is supported by this strut, known as the V-link.

Tilt
Behind this panel, the motor drives the joint that tilts the robot arm forward and backward.

UX 120

Robot arm
A robot arm can be programmed to perform different welding and handling tasks in factories. This particular robot is used to join pieces of metal. Heat and pressure created by an electric current make the metal fuse. This process is called spot welding.

Not in a tangle
A hanger and stand keep the welding pipes untangled and out of the way.

In control
Control cables carry the signals for positioning the robot's various joints. The end effector has its own separate control cable.

Programming off-line
To get assembly line robots working together, they may be pre-programmed at a remote computer terminal. The program is then transferred to the robot's controller. This is called off-line programming.

Twist at the waist
At the waist joint, the whole robot rotates around its base, which is bolted to the floor.

Control cable
As well as the air, water, and electricity pipes, there is the control cable, taking signals between the controller and the end effector.

Spot-welding

A spot-welding robot in action looks very dramatic. Spot-welding requires short but intense bursts of power. For spot-welding car parts, about 300 car batteries' worth of power is needed for a single spot-weld, taking just half a second.

Rotating wrist
The wrist area comprises three joints. This one allows the wrist to rotate.

Side to side
This wrist joint moves the welding gun from side to side.

Raising and lowering
This wrist joint moves the spot-welding gun up and down.

Positions, please
Each motor includes a device that sends signals back to the controller, stating where that joint has moved to. This is called positional feedback.

Guns and arms
The spot-welding gun is the robot's end effector. It has two arms. They end in electrodes that apply the current that fuses the metal together.

The remote
The detachable teach pendant has a screen that shows the state of the robot's program and a set of buttons for controlling the robot's movement.

Hotter and hotter
The current passing between the electrodes can raise the temperature of the metal to 1,500 °F (800°C).

Controller

Many factory robots have controllers that can be situated away from the robot itself. Industrial robots may be stationary but the controller can be wheeled around or taken elsewhere for maintenance or reprogramming.

Go-between
This piece of electronics sends signals and commands to the robot's end effector, under instruction from the main processing unit.

Processing unit
This is the main processing unit, which contains the robot's program.

Servo controller
The servo controller takes information and commands from the main processor. It converts them into signals that the servo power blocks understand.

Direct action

A robot may be taught how to move by a human operator guiding it through its exact movements. This is the case with many spray-painting robots. It is known as direct teaching or walk-through programming.

Mains transformer
A transformer ensures the controller can be connected to the electricity supply whatever the voltage, which varies from country to country.

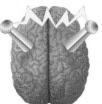

Artificial intelligence

If a computer, robot, or any other machine has the power to think and act without intervention, it has artificial intelligence (AI). There are many areas of AI research. One is building robot systems that can perform human-styled actions such as moving, seeing, and touching in an intelligent way. Another important area is building computers and programs that get closer and closer to thinking in a human way. Researchers find it useful to try out the AI abilities of their robots in practical games.

Tight defense
In a defensive situation, ball-following and collision-avoidance cause the robots to form a semicircle around the ball.

Attack again
If a circle is formed around the ball, the robot facing forward will try to bat the ball to the side so that one of the others can advance it.

Eye on the ball
The goalkeeper's second vision system monitors the ball. The robot is programmed to move to the right or left to knock the ball away from the goal.

Robot keeper
The robot goalkeeper has two vision systems. The one in the rear watches the goal line to make sure the keeper remains properly in front of the goal.

Looking forward
Each field robot has seven sonar sensors, known as pingers, on the front and sides. These provide information about objects that the robot must avoid.

A learning game
The RoboCup soccer competition for teams of robots was developed by researchers. Playing soccer as a team provides robots with a tough test. The environment is fast-moving and constantly changing. This team of robots, called the Spirit of Bolivia, exhibits aspects of intelligence by learning from the events on the field around them and by cooperating with one another to perform a task.

Push, bat, or whirl
The robots are not allowed to hold the ball. They push it forward or bat it to the side with their gripper arms, or whirl to "kick" it with their rear end.

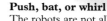

Miss it!
The sonar pingers are positioned above the height of the ball. This is so that the robots can detect and avoid other robots and walls.

Right size
The ball is 8 in (20 cm) in diameter and a single color for easy identification by the robots' vision sensors.

Gap sensors
The mouse is equipped with sensors that detect gaps or openings in the walls.

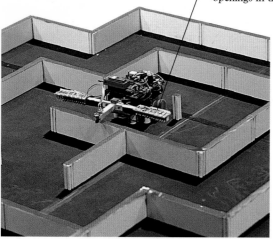

Micro mazes
Mazes created especially for mobile robots are one popular test of limited artificial intelligence. The robot, known as a mouse, must navigate its way out of the maze as quickly as possible. Micro-maze competitions between different robots have been run for many years.

Get a grip
Each of the robot's grippers has a sensor on the end to detect whether it is touching anything. To prevent ball-holding, which is not allowed, a box can be placed between the grippers.

Color sense

The vision system can be trained to recognize up to three colors at one time. It also sends information on the size, shape, and location of these colored objects to the robot's onboard controller.

Checkmate

With its complex strategy, chess has been used as a test of computer intelligence. IBM's Deep Blue computer beat the World Chess Champion Gary Kasparov in a series of games in 1997.

Assessing the competition
Deep Blue attempts to analyze its opponent's moves and discover his strategy.

Making up its mind
Deep Blue can run thousands of potential moves through its program to determine the most advantageous one.

Robots like us

No one is sure yet whether a robot can ever be built with true, full artificial human intelligence, like the androids of science fiction. Scientists and engineers continue their work to create one.

Robbie the Robot
Super-intelligent robots, like Robbie the Robot from the movie *Forbidden Planet*, are still to be developed.

Know the game
Even when the ball is at the far end of the field, the goalkeeper robot "knows" to stay on the line.

Team spirit

The robots cooperate as a team whether in attack or in defense. Each robot tries to get between the ball and its own goal and then move the ball toward the opponents' goal. Sonar-based collision-avoidance causes the robots to fall into formations, and they are even capable of attempting to pass to one another.

Pioneer 1

The field players of the Spirit of Bolivia are adapted Pioneer 1 robots. The Pioneer 1 is a low-cost mobile robot used by many research and education establishments. At 18 in (45 cm) by 14 in (35 cm), they play in RoboCup's middle-sized league.

Antenna
Pioneer can "talk to" a computer or a human operator using its radio modem.

Color cam
The video camera works in color. It is fixed in position, but wide-angled.

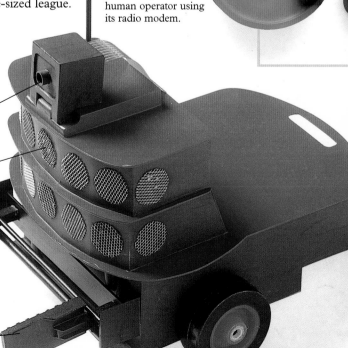

Attack formation
In an offensive situation, one robot pushes the ball while others follow, ready to recover it if it is stolen or fumbled. The robots can move surprisingly fast. Their top speed is 35 in (90 cm) per second both forward and backward.

Sonar pingers
Each of the seven sonar systems consists of a transmitter and a receiver.

Extendable grippers
Pioneer's grippers can move in and out to grasp an object, although for RoboCup they are fixed in one position.

AGV systems

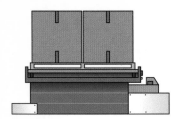

When a factory robot has a stationary base, it is easy to know its "working envelope." A robot's working envelope is the area it takes up, including the full extent its end effector can reach in all directions. When a robot is mobile, it is not as easy to define its working envelope and so keep people and equipment out of the way. One solution is to use automated guided vehicles (AGVs). These run along specified routes controlled by navigation systems and sensors. AGVs are driverless and are used for handling and moving industrial materials or products in a factory.

Robot trolley
AGVs are one type of mobile robot with automatic guidance. This amazing robot supermarket trolley is another. It uses an ultrasound system to follow a customer at a distance of 2 ft 4 in (70 cm) as he or she wanders around the store.

On the production line
The FLD 1604 is a specialized forklift AGV used to transport large objects around a factory. Powered by a large electrical battery, it can move backward and forward along its guide path for up to 16 hours before its battery needs recharging. Apart from its guiding navigation, it has a number of other safety features.

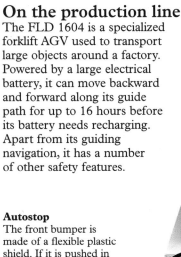

Autostop
The front bumper is made of a flexible plastic shield. If it is pushed in by an object, the AGV automatically stops.

Start up
Once the bumper is back in its normal position, the AGV automatically starts up again after a five-second delay.

A lot of toothpaste
A container weighing up to 3.2 tons (3,550 kg), transports toothpaste from giant mixers to the filling line.

Bumper surprise
Sensors on the rear bumpers come into use when the AGV is in reverse and when it is not carrying a load. On the inside edge of each bumper, there is an infrared transmitter or receiver. An infrared beam passes between them.

Breaking the beam
If the infrared beam passing between the rear bumpers is broken by an object in the way, a signal is triggered and the AGV stops.

Safe routes
The painted lines, called clearways, show workers the working envelope of the AGV and warn them to keep clear.

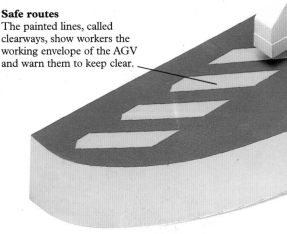

AGV in action
Although some AGVs are used in offices to deliver mail or in hospitals to transport bedding and medicines, the majority can be found in factories. This German AGV transports components between different machining stages. It is an important link in keeping the factory running automatically.

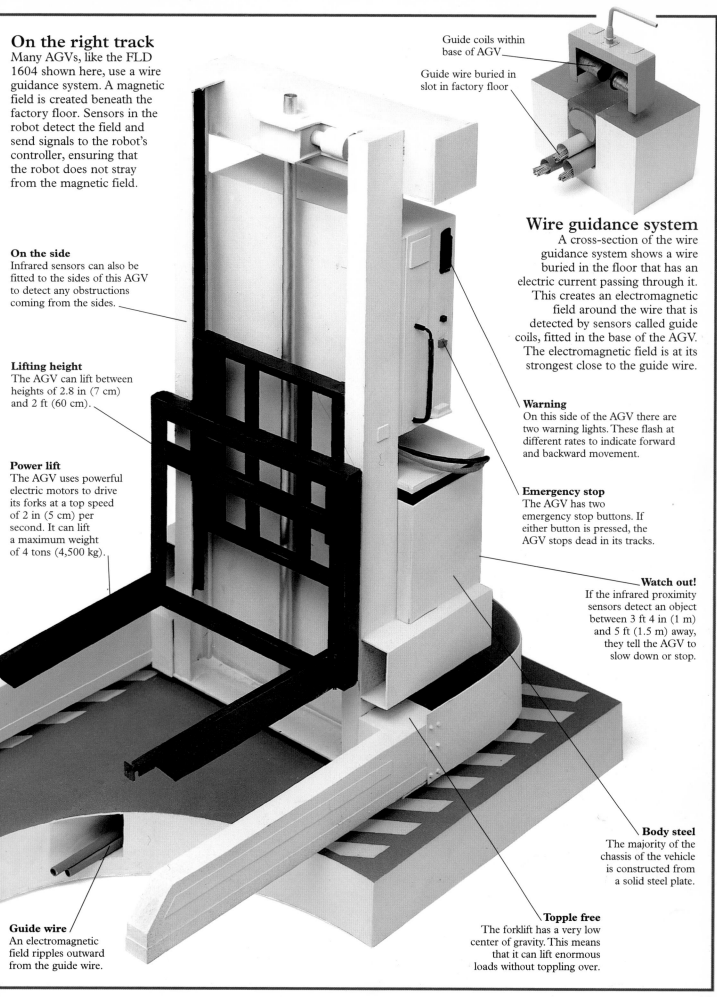

On the right track

Many AGVs, like the FLD 1604 shown here, use a wire guidance system. A magnetic field is created beneath the factory floor. Sensors in the robot detect the field and send signals to the robot's controller, ensuring that the robot does not stray from the magnetic field.

On the side
Infrared sensors can also be fitted to the sides of this AGV to detect any obstructions coming from the sides.

Lifting height
The AGV can lift between heights of 2.8 in (7 cm) and 2 ft (60 cm).

Power lift
The AGV uses powerful electric motors to drive its forks at a top speed of 2 in (5 cm) per second. It can lift a maximum weight of 4 tons (4,500 kg).

Guide wire
An electromagnetic field ripples outward from the guide wire.

Guide coils within base of AGV

Guide wire buried in slot in factory floor

Wire guidance system
A cross-section of the wire guidance system shows a wire buried in the floor that has an electric current passing through it. This creates an electromagnetic field around the wire that is detected by sensors called guide coils, fitted in the base of the AGV. The electromagnetic field is at its strongest close to the guide wire.

Warning
On this side of the AGV there are two warning lights. These flash at different rates to indicate forward and backward movement.

Emergency stop
The AGV has two emergency stop buttons. If either button is pressed, the AGV stops dead in its tracks.

Watch out!
If the infrared proximity sensors detect an object between 3 ft 4 in (1 m) and 5 ft (1.5 m) away, they tell the AGV to slow down or stop.

Body steel
The majority of the chassis of the vehicle is constructed from a solid steel plate.

Topple free
The forklift has a very low center of gravity. This means that it can lift enormous loads without toppling over.

Difficult terrain

Wheels are fine for robots moving around on flat, smooth, factory floors. But how does a robot move over a rough, unpredictable surface such as rocky ground or inside a damaged building? Some robots have tracks, similar to tanks, but many robots have legs, providing far more freedom to move over difficult terrain. A small number of robots have two legs and are called bipeds. Unlike humans, who have a sophisticated balancing system, biped robots find it hard to remain stable. So most robots designed for difficult terrain come with four or more legs.

Vacuum suction gripper under foot

Joint of main body

Robug II

First steps
This six-legged robot was built to research the way robots learn to walk using artificial intelligence. It can also be preprogrammed to walk in a certain way.

Air pressure gauge

Scaling the wall
Robug II has four legs and can walk up walls. Its body is in two parts, jointed in the middle, allowing it to move from the horizontal to the vertical. The research involved in Robug II helped develop Robug III.

Computer power
Robug III is connected via this data cable to a program run on a personal computer. The program instructs the robot to perform different walking gaits.

Leg control
Each leg has its own microprocessor. These are all connected to the data cable, and so to the computer.

Strong and light
Robug weighs 132 lbs (60 kg). Much of its body is made of a lightweight but strong material called carbon fiber.

Heavy loads
Robug III can drag loads of 221 lbs (100 kg) both along the ground and up the wall.

Vacuum suction
Robug III's feet grip surfaces, attaching the robot to walls and even ceilings, using vacuum suction. A vacuum is an area that is largely empty of any matter.

Rubber seal
Each foot has a rubber seal. Once this is placed on a surface, a venturi pump installed in each leg draws out most of the air from under the foot, creating a vacuum.

Outside pressure
The pressure of air on the foot from outside helps create the suction, causing the foot to grip the surface firmly.

How fast?
Robug III's current top speed is 4 in (10 cm) a second.

Horizontal to vertical

The way in which a robot operates its legs to move is called its walking gait. The Robug team has studied insect walking gaits and developed computer simulations to work out the best way for Robug III to move. The robot can be programmed to move using different gaits. This simulation shows it moving from the roof to the wall.

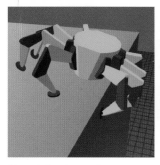

Step 1: horizontal

Step 2: on an angle

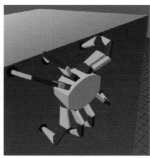

Step 3: vertical

Delicate steps
Each leg can move on its own. So if a stone lies in the path of one leg, that leg can contract to rise over the stone without tilting the whole robot.

Air compressor link
Robug III is linked to a 5.5-kw air compressor, providing the power to move its legs and to create the suction under its feet. This is called pneumatic power.

Redundant joint
Robug III can climb at an angle and cross difficult terrain while keeping its body close to the ground. The redundant joint allows it to do this.

Boldly go forth
Robug III is an eight-legged robot designed to move around hazardous, unpredictable environments. These include the inside of a nuclear reactor or an area affected by a radioactive accident. The robot can be used to move debris, as well as to investigate unidentified substances. It can also be attached with an arm, which can be used, for example, to rescue injured persons.

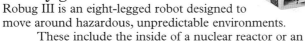

Crab or spider
Robug's eight-legged shape looks a bit like a crab or a spider. The Robug team studied insects to come up with the robot's practical and versatile design.

Multijointed
Each of the robot's eight legs has four joints. The joints can operate independently or the whole leg can be lifted as a rigid structure.

Fitting instruments
Video cameras, a laser range finder, Geiger counters – which measure radiation – and other sensors can be fitted to the robot's body.

Stepping clear
Legged robots are useful in the nuclear industry, where a robot has to clamber over pipes and other equipment to investigate a possible radiation leak. This inspection robot, called Robin, has six legs and is remote controlled. Here Robin is lifting the lid off a steel drum.

Quite a size
Robug III is 31 in (80 cm) long and 24 in (60 cm) wide, with a height of 24 in (60 cm).

Power of vision

Some mobile robots are fitted with television cameras that send images back to a manned control base. These robots can obtain pictures from places where a human cannot go, such as inside a burning building or on another planet. Other robots use a form of vision as a sensor to determine their surroundings. How a robot sees, though, is usually quite different from how the human eye works.

Robart III

Designed to patrol offices and warehouses, Robart III is a security robot that uses a large range of sensors to "see" intruders and a gun that fires tranquilizing darts to immobilize them. Unlike a human security guard, it will never fall asleep, perform an "inside job," or be easily overcome by intruders.

Going through the motions
The motion detector not only instructs the head to move so that the video continues to track an intruder, but also angles the gun, using this joint, to point at the intruder.

Magic darts
Robart III's main weapon is a six-barreled nonlethal dart gun. Different types of darts, including tranquilizer darts, can be used.

Turning barrels
The six barrels rotate so that one is always in line with the pneumatic power that fires the dart. To fire all six darts takes just 1.5 seconds.

Pressurized accumulator
A computer-controlled valve between the accumulator and the gun opens just long enough to exert the pressure needed for a dart to be fired.

Hose for air
Air from the air bottle passes via a hose to the pressurized accumulator.

Control
The gun's functions are controlled via signals sent through these cables.

Captured on video
The video camera sends its black-and-white pictures both to a human operator and internally to the onboard motion detector.

Proximity detector

Collared
The collar has infrared motion detectors all the way around it. It is these detectors that first alert Robart to a possible intruder.

Motion dedector

Robot guide dog

Robots have even been designed to provide automated eyes for people with vision difficulties. Guidecane, a prototype robot, uses a ring of ultrasonic sensors to detect and steer around obstacles, guiding the user as it goes.

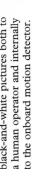

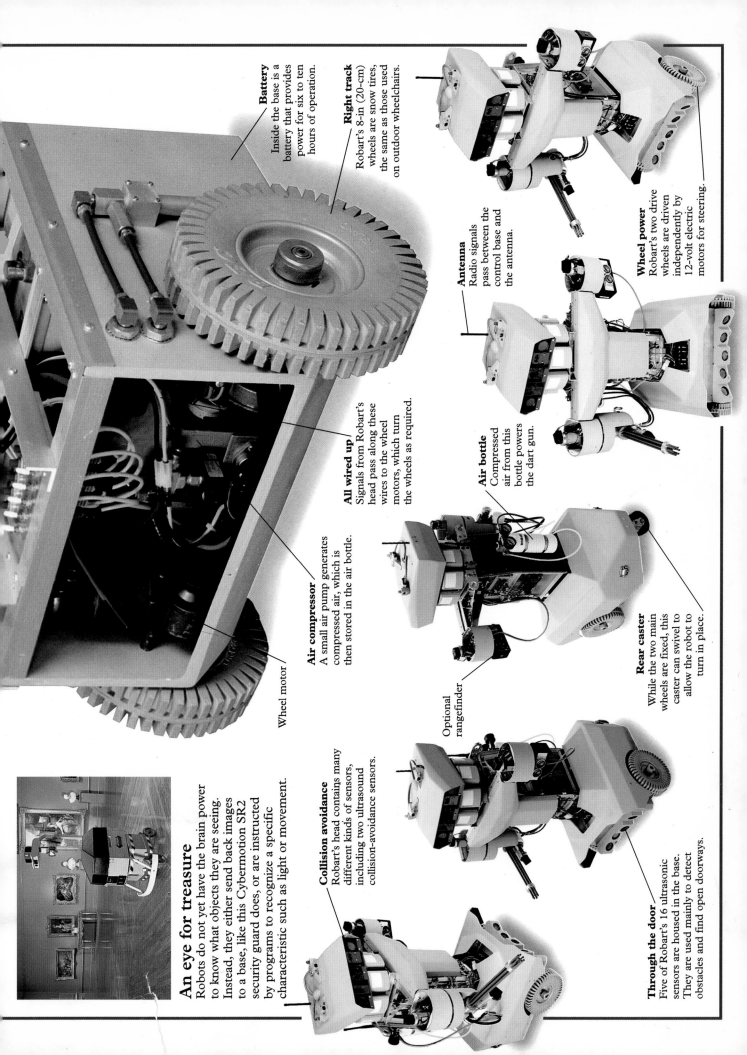

Battery
Inside the base is a battery that provides power for six to ten hours of operation.

Right track
Robart's 8-in (20-cm) wheels are snow tires, the same as those used on outdoor wheelchairs.

Antenna
Radio signals pass between the control base and the antenna.

Wheel power
Robart's two drive wheels are driven independently by 12-volt electric motors for steering.

All wired up
Signals from Robart's head pass along these wires to the wheel motors, which turn the wheels as required.

Air compressor
A small air pump generates compressed air, which is then stored in the air bottle.

Air bottle
Compressed air from this bottle powers the dart gun.

Wheel motor

Optional rangefinder

Rear caster
While the two main wheels are fixed, this caster can swivel to allow the robot to turn in place.

An eye for treasure

Robots do not yet have the brain power to know what objects they are seeing. Instead, they either send back images to a base, like this Cybermotion SR2 security guard does, or are instructed by programs to recognize a specific characteristic such as light or movement.

Collision avoidance
Robart's head contains many different kinds of sensors, including two ultrasound collision-avoidance sensors.

Through the door
Five of Robart's 16 ultrasonic sensors are housed in the base. They are used mainly to detect obstacles and find open doorways.

Performing surgery

Although mobile robots have been helping out in hospitals for some time, it is only recently that they have been assisting in the operating room. Even the best surgeon cannot move as accurately as an advanced robot arm. One day, it may be possible for a surgeon to "perform" an operation hundreds or thousands of miles away from the patient. Using virtual reality, a surgeon would go through the operation. The procedure would be relayed, possibly via satellite, to the surgical robot, which may have its own human assistant.

Mini surgical robot
Cleo is a prototype surgical robot that is small enough to fit inside an adult's colon. Equipped with a claw, antennae, and sensors, it may in future be used to operate on a patient's colon internally.

Route planner
Helpmate has a computer-controlled "map" of the hospital it is working in.

Bumper
A variety of sensors ensures that the robot does not bump into people or furniture.

Robot orderlies
Mobile robots can be found in some hospitals acting as orderlies, carrying patients their medical supplies. This Helpmate can even use elevators to travel around. It carries up to 198 lbs (90 kg) of medicines, records, or blankets.

Robodoc
One of the first robot surgeons to perform part of an operation on humans is a hip surgery robot called Robodoc. It takes its instructions from Orthodoc, a computer work station that is preprogrammed with a plan of the operation. It drills an extremely accurate hole in the patient's femur, into which the hip implant fits.

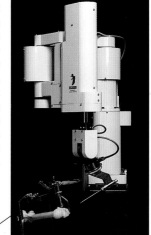

Highly successful
Robodoc has already performed over 1,000 operations on human patients.

Holding still
The clamp, called a femur fixator, holds the leg firmly in place.

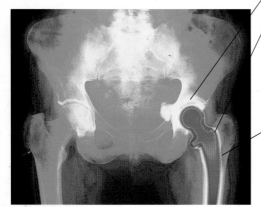

Hip socket

A hair's breadth
The gap between bone and implant must be less than 0.01 in (0.25 mm) – half the thickness of a human hair.

Femur

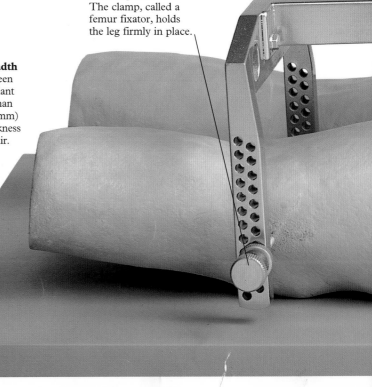

Get hip!
Many hip replacement operations use a long-lasting, cementless implant made of steel or titanium. The surrounding bone is tricked into thinking that the implant also is bone. So the bone grows into the implant's slightly porous surface.

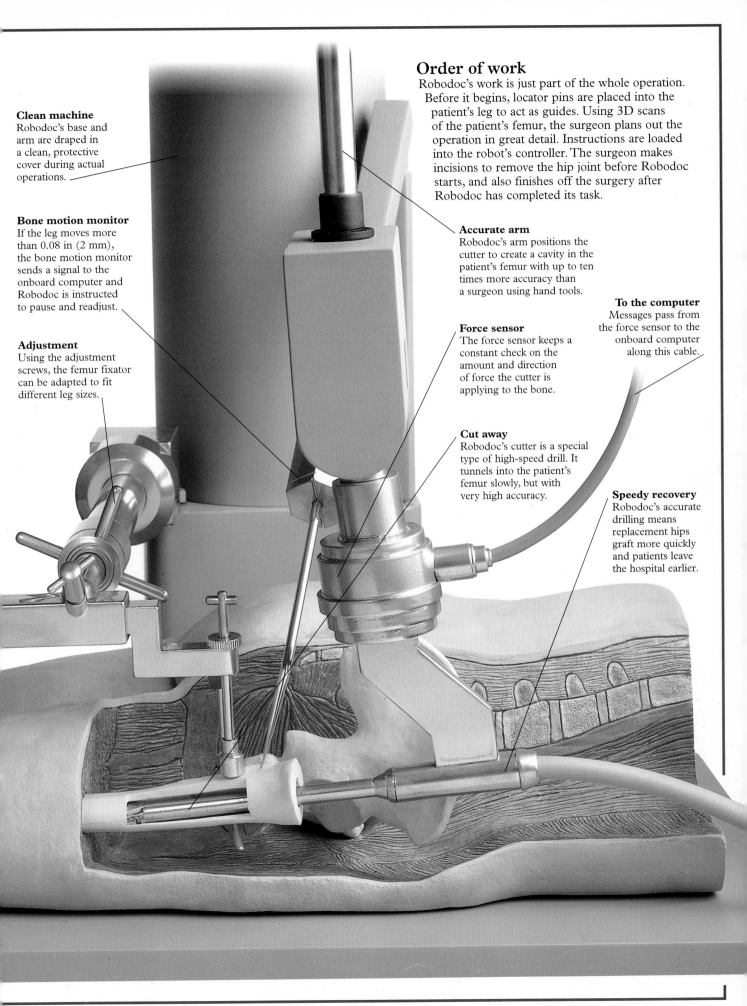

Clean machine
Robodoc's base and arm are draped in a clean, protective cover during actual operations.

Bone motion monitor
If the leg moves more than 0.08 in (2 mm), the bone motion monitor sends a signal to the onboard computer and Robodoc is instructed to pause and readjust.

Adjustment
Using the adjustment screws, the femur fixator can be adapted to fit different leg sizes.

Order of work
Robodoc's work is just part of the whole operation. Before it begins, locator pins are placed into the patient's leg to act as guides. Using 3D scans of the patient's femur, the surgeon plans out the operation in great detail. Instructions are loaded into the robot's controller. The surgeon makes incisions to remove the hip joint before Robodoc starts, and also finishes off the surgery after Robodoc has completed its task.

Accurate arm
Robodoc's arm positions the cutter to create a cavity in the patient's femur with up to ten times more accuracy than a surgeon using hand tools.

Force sensor
The force sensor keeps a constant check on the amount and direction of force the cutter is applying to the bone.

Cut away
Robodoc's cutter is a special type of high-speed drill. It tunnels into the patient's femur slowly, but with very high accuracy.

To the computer
Messages pass from the force sensor to the onboard computer along this cable.

Speedy recovery
Robodoc's accurate drilling means replacement hips graft more quickly and patients leave the hospital earlier.

Sheep shearing

Much farm work is repetitive and tiring – ideal for robots. Farm robots need to be tough yet not damage livestock or crops. Unlike the manufactured materials handled by factory robots, every sheep, cow, and turnip is a different shape and size. This makes the success of the sheep-shearing robot Shear Magic all the more amazing. Its designers had to overcome many problems, such as holding a struggling sheep firmly but safely. It works with an automated cradle to load and unload the sheep, and uses various sensors that keep the clippers away from the skin, while still getting a close cut.

Hard work
Sheep shearing by hand is a very skilled job, with difficult and painful work. The stresses on backs and joints are great. A robot shearer may not be able to shear faster than a human, but it could save a lot of injuries.

Painstaking business
The shearer uses mechanical clippers to cut the wool, while simultaneously holding the sheep and stretching the skin.

Electric wool
Wool has conductive properties. It can carry different amounts of electricity, depending on environmental factors. This can confuse the robot's sensors, which was another problem to be overcome by the Shear Magic team.

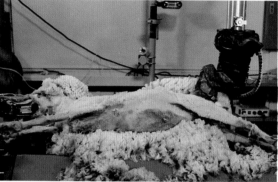

Shear Magic
The Shear Magic robot operates from above the sheep and can move along tracks in the ceiling, giving it an extra degree of freedom. These tracks can be built to run the length of a barn, enabling a line of sheep to be sheared one after the other.

A clean cut
Shear Magic's cutter mechanism, shown in this simplified model, uses an advanced software model of the surface of the sheep. As the cutter gets close to shearing, its sensors take over.

Robot milking
Robots can be used for other jobs on the farm besides shearing. Every year farmers spend 90,000 hours attaching cows to milking machines in Britain alone. This robot milker, a research project, can milk cows without human assistance.

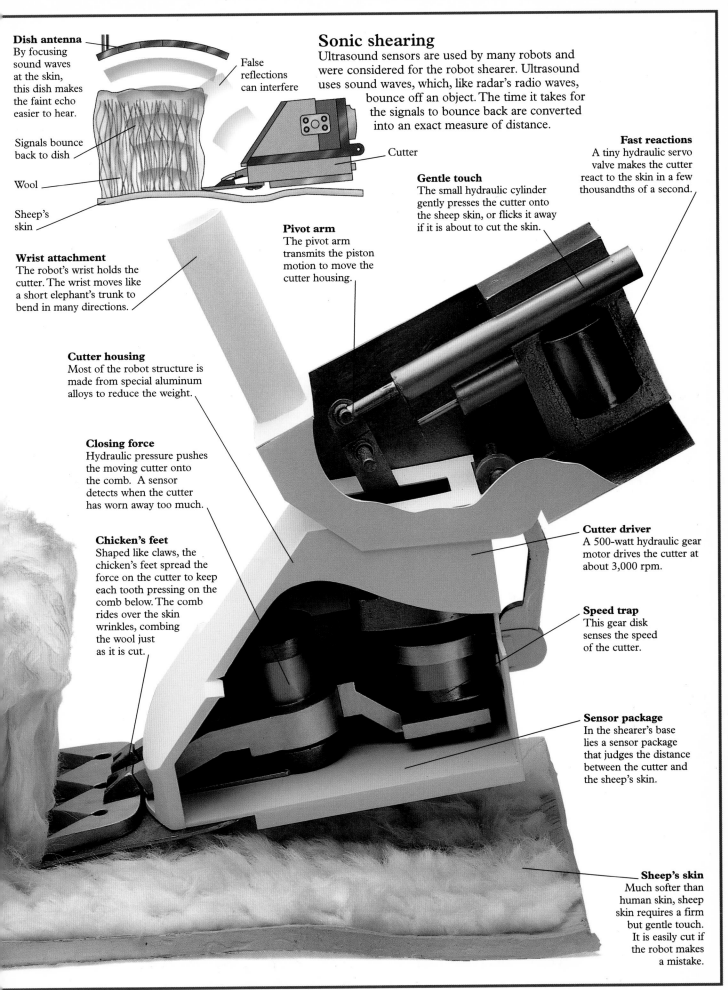

Dish antenna
By focusing sound waves at the skin, this dish makes the faint echo easier to hear.

Signals bounce back to dish

Wool

Sheep's skin

False reflections can interfere

Cutter

Sonic shearing

Ultrasound sensors are used by many robots and were considered for the robot shearer. Ultrasound uses sound waves, which, like radar's radio waves, bounce off an object. The time it takes for the signals to bounce back are converted into an exact measure of distance.

Fast reactions
A tiny hydraulic servo valve makes the cutter react to the skin in a few thousandths of a second.

Gentle touch
The small hydraulic cylinder gently presses the cutter onto the sheep skin, or flicks it away if it is about to cut the skin.

Pivot arm
The pivot arm transmits the piston motion to move the cutter housing.

Wrist attachment
The robot's wrist holds the cutter. The wrist moves like a short elephant's trunk to bend in many directions.

Cutter housing
Most of the robot structure is made from special aluminum alloys to reduce the weight.

Closing force
Hydraulic pressure pushes the moving cutter onto the comb. A sensor detects when the cutter has worn away too much.

Chicken's feet
Shaped like claws, the chicken's feet spread the force on the cutter to keep each tooth pressing on the comb below. The comb rides over the skin wrinkles, combing the wool just as it is cut.

Cutter driver
A 500-watt hydraulic gear motor drives the cutter at about 3,000 rpm.

Speed trap
This gear disk senses the speed of the cutter.

Sensor package
In the shearer's base lies a sensor package that judges the distance between the cutter and the sheep's skin.

Sheep's skin
Much softer than human skin, sheep skin requires a firm but gentle touch. It is easily cut if the robot makes a mistake.

Exploring space

Space is a hostile environment. We can send human beings into it, but not for as long or as far as we would like to. When they do go, astronauts need huge amounts of equipment – from oxygen-filled living quarters (with toilets that will work in zero gravity) to supplies of food, water, and oxygen. Robots do not require these things, so they are popular for space missions, both to other planets and on space shuttles and future space stations. Human spacewalks are time-consuming and hazardous. Flying robots, complete with cameras, could cut down the number of spacewalks needed on a mission.

Ready to launch
NASA's first roving space camera, shown here in the space shuttle's cargo bay, is called AERCam Sprint. At 14 in (35 cm) in diameter, Sprint is about the same size as a beach ball, but weighs a lot more, 35 lbs (16 kg).

Illuminating
Sprint's powerful floodlight is the same as those used in astronauts' helmets.

Camera
Sprint has two miniature color television cameras with lenses of 0.2 in (6 mm) and 0.5 in (12 mm).

Camera

Free flyer
Sprint has six degrees of freedom and, using its 12 thrusters, can free fly in any direction. The thrusters also act as stabilizers by emitting small power bursts.

Bright lights
There are six flashing yellow lights fitted to Sprint, making it visible in darkness.

Slow speed
Sprint travels at a slow speed of 1.7 mph (2.7 kph), which, together with its cushioned outer surface, helps prevent any damage if it bumps into other equipment.

Thruster

First mission
Sprint's first mission was aboard the 87th space shuttle flight in November 1997. During its successful, 76-minute flight, it was tele-operated from within the space shuttle by astronaut Steve Lindsey. Future versions will be able to fly and navigate autonomously (all by themselves).

Soft surface
Sprint's surface is covered in a layer of cushioned Nomex felt, 0.6 in (1.5 cm) deep. To avoid wrinkles, the felt is affixed in panels, similar to a soccer ball.

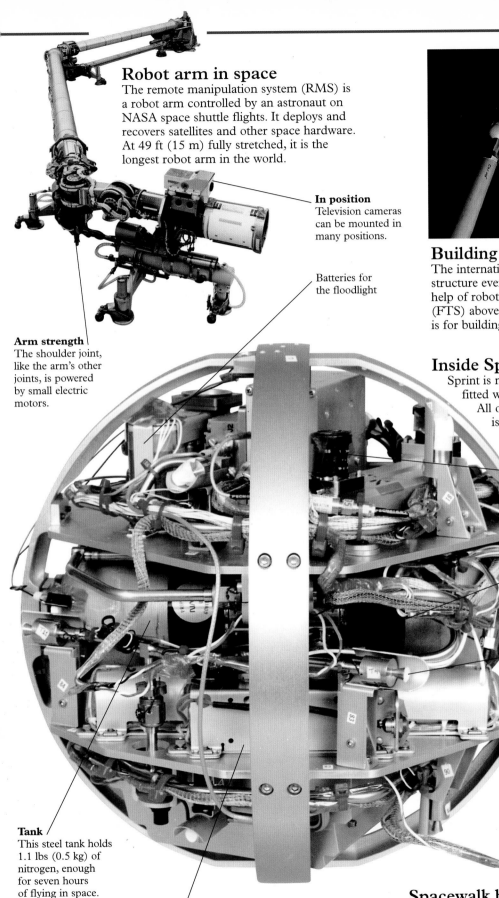

Robot arm in space

The remote manipulation system (RMS) is a robot arm controlled by an astronaut on NASA space shuttle flights. It deploys and recovers satellites and other space hardware. At 49 ft (15 m) fully stretched, it is the longest robot arm in the world.

In position
Television cameras can be mounted in many positions.

Batteries for the floodlight

Arm strength
The shoulder joint, like the arm's other joints, is powered by small electric motors.

Building in space

The international space station, the largest structure ever to be built in space, will require the help of robots. NASA's flight telerobotic servicer (FTS) above, with its gripping hand end effector, is for building and maintaining the space station.

Inside Sprint

Sprint is made up of two hoops or rings, fitted with an upper and lower shelf. All of Sprint's equipment is fitted to these shelves.

Camera
The television signals from Sprint's cameras are sent back to the controller in the shuttle.

Regulator
Two regulators feed the thrusters with the exact amount of nitrogen at the right pressure.

Thruster
Each thruster is powered by nitrogen from its internal tank.

No strings attached
When the cover is in place, this electrical wire connects to one of the radio antennas, which send and receive signals. No cables attach Sprint to its controller.

Tank
This steel tank holds 1.1 lbs (0.5 kg) of nitrogen, enough for seven hours of flying in space.

Batteries
Sprint's electronics are powered by lithium batteries, lasting up to seven hours.

Spacewalk helper

The RMS arm can handle loads up to 26.6 tons (29,500 kg) in weight, so an astronaut can be carried with ease. On this space shuttle flight, an astronaut is using the arm as a mobile platform to transport him safely above the cargo bay.

Missions on Mars

Robot probes reached both the Moon and Mars before man. Robots do not need food and water, or bringing back once their mission is completed. Unlike lunar probes, robots on Mars need to be able to work by themselves. This is mainly due to the huge distances involved. A radio signal to the Moon can take only a few seconds, but even at its closest orbit point, Mars is 34 million miles (55 million kilometers) away from the Earth, 140 times farther away than the Moon. Signals take about 20 minutes to travel from the Earth to Mars and back – far too long for a mobile robot to be tele-operated.

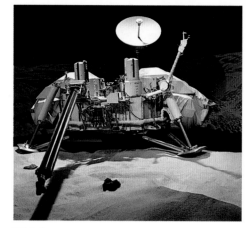

Viking 1
The first probe to visit Mars' surface was *Viking 1*. Its telescopic robot arm had a small scoop on the end to collect soil samples. *Viking 1* analyzed these samples and sent back details to Earth. The image above is an engineering model of *Viking 1*.

Mars *Sojourner*
NASA's *Sojourner* was the first robot to rove around another planet, taking photographs and investigating rocks and soil. It moved at a speed of 0.4 in (1 cm) per second and was built to survive the hostile environment of Mars, where temperatures range from 60°F (17°C) to -180°F to (-120°C).

Keeping steady
If *Sojourner* had toppled over, the mission would have ended. As soon as the robot began to tilt, motion sensors on its sides sent signals to the controller to stop the robot.

Rock composition
The alpha proton X-ray spectrometer (APXS) was used to study the composition of rocks on Mars.

Fun in the sun
Pathfinder's side panels were called petals. They unfolded on landing to let *Sojourner* out and then generated solar energy.

Pathfinder and *Sojourner*
Sojourner was carried by the *Pathfinder* probe on a seven-month journey to Mars. Landing on July 4, 1997, *Sojourner* had no direct link with mission control on Earth. Instead, it sent back signals to *Pathfinder*, which relayed them back to Earth.

Steel grip
The tread of the wheel was made of stainless steel and had tiny studs to provide extra grip.

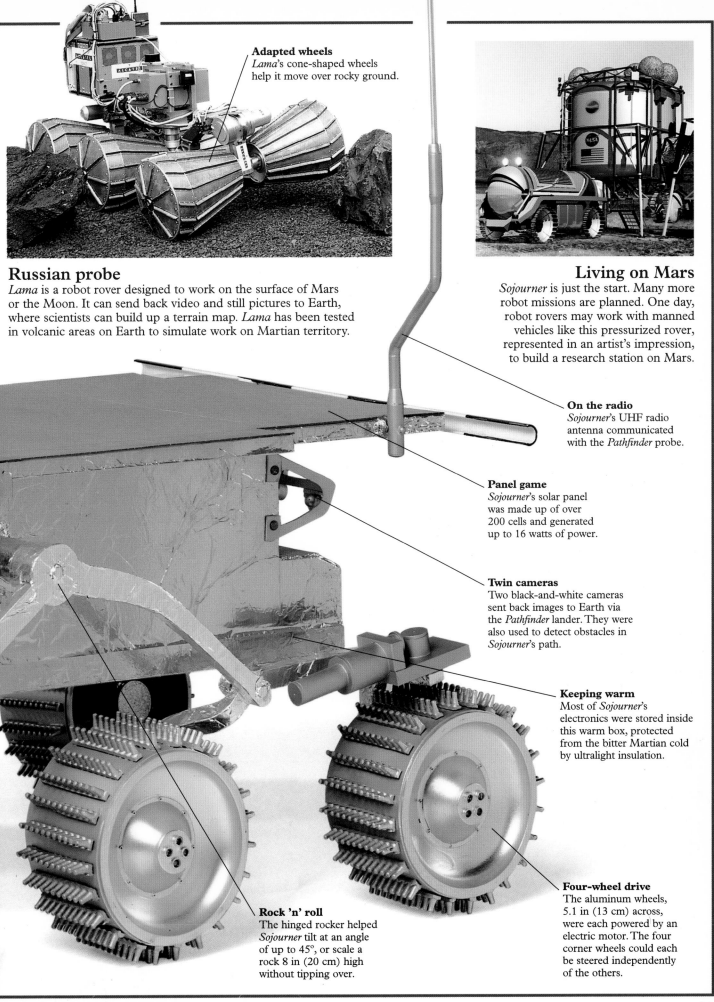

Russian probe

Lama is a robot rover designed to work on the surface of Mars or the Moon. It can send back video and still pictures to Earth, where scientists can build up a terrain map. *Lama* has been tested in volcanic areas on Earth to simulate work on Martian territory.

Adapted wheels
Lama's cone-shaped wheels help it move over rocky ground.

Living on Mars

Sojourner is just the start. Many more robot missions are planned. One day, robot rovers may work with manned vehicles like this pressurized rover, represented in an artist's impression, to build a research station on Mars.

On the radio
Sojourner's UHF radio antenna communicated with the *Pathfinder* probe.

Panel game
Sojourner's solar panel was made up of over 200 cells and generated up to 16 watts of power.

Twin cameras
Two black-and-white cameras sent back images to Earth via the *Pathfinder* lander. They were also used to detect obstacles in *Sojourner*'s path.

Keeping warm
Most of *Sojourner*'s electronics were stored inside this warm box, protected from the bitter Martian cold by ultralight insulation.

Rock 'n' roll
The hinged rocker helped *Sojourner* tilt at an angle of up to 45°, or scale a rock 8 in (20 cm) high without tipping over.

Four-wheel drive
The aluminum wheels, 5.1 in (13 cm) across, were each powered by an electric motor. The four corner wheels could each be steered independently of the others.

Working underwater

Underwater robots perform all kinds of useful jobs and can withstand water pressure far better than a human diver. Most human divers cannot go deeper than 328 ft (100 m), whereas robots can go forty times as deep. There are two types of underwater robots: tele-operated (pp. 36–37) vehicles; and autonomous underwater vehicles (AUVs), which operate without constant orders from humans. AUVs are programmed in advance to perform a set of tasks.

Autosub

Autosub is an AUV designed to carry out many kinds of scientific research missions. Shaped like a fat torpedo, it can carry different scientific payloads. Autosub could act as a roving detector for environmental hazards, or as an exploration vessel for oil, gas, and minerals.

Power switch for batteries

Power switch for vehicle systems

Emergency drill
An abort weight of 66 lbs (30 kg) of steel, attached by an electromagnet, is connected to the computer network. If there is a problem, such as a leak, the magnet switches off, the weight drops, and Autosub rises to the surface.

Cargo bay
Scientific instruments for each mission are placed in the nose of the vehicle. The bay is 35 cubic feet (1 cubic meter) in size and can hold up to 220 lbs (100 kg) in weight.

Keeping track
A flashing light provides a visual guide when Autosub surfaces. Inside it is a satellite beacon to enable the support ship to locate the vehicle.

Computer network
The microprocessors are all connected through a network to form a "distributed" control and monitoring system. Mission control is also on the network.

Lookout
The forward-looking sonar uses sound waves to detect obstructions ahead.

Microprocessors
Each scientific instrument and vehicle control unit has its own microprocessor.

Speed
The acoustic doppler current profiler (ADCP) measures the speed Autosub travels both through the water and across the seabed. This enables currents to be calculated.

Conductivity instrument
An electric field is created by this conductivity instrument. The water's resistance to this field indicates the amount of salt in the water, which reveals more about the water currents. The instrument also measures water temperature.

Depth
The ADCP also calculates the depth of the water and can ensure that the vehicle does not hit the bottom.

History underwater
Built by the US Navy, the advanced unmanned search system (AUSS) discovered this Douglas Skyraider night fighter from the Korean War during a 3,937-ft (1,200-m) test dive.

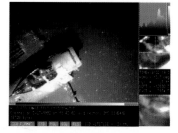

In action

Autosub uses the Global Positioning System (GPS) to navigate on the surface. It receives a signal from a number of GPS satellites to compute its location.

Radio in
A radio modem connects Autosub to its support ship on the water's surface.

Propeller

Stern planes

pH probe
Extending down through Autosub's frame, this probe measures the water's pH level.

Buoyancy
Despite weighing 3,087 lbs (1,400 kg) out of the water, Autosub has enough buoyancy to prevent it sinking to the bottom. The buoyancy is provided by foam panels in the midsection.

Emergency acoustic beacon for locating Autosub should it sink to the bottom

Attitude sensor
This device monitors Autosub's position, its rate of pitch and roll, and the direction in which it is traveling.

What next?
The mission controller contains a series of preprogrammed commands, such as how fast or deep Autosub should dive, which the vehicle executes in order to perform its mission.

Battery power
Batteries provide Autosub with its power. It uses either seven car batteries to give it a range of 43 miles (70 km) or an astonishing 2,200 flashlight batteries, which allow it to travel 137 miles (220 km).

A good size
Autosub is 23 ft (7 m) long and 3 ft (0.9 m) in diameter.

Alvin on the surface
Alvin was used to investigate the wreck of the *Titanic*. Alvin launched Jason Jr to perform the search 3,965 m (13,009 ft) below the ocean's surface, at a pressure 400 times greater than at sea level.

Clothed in lycra
The robot fish's skin is made from strong, flexible lycra material.

Sink or swim

The Robotuna is modeled on the bluefin tuna fish, a highly efficient swimmer. Six motors are connected to internal tendons that flex the body back and forth so that the robot swims just like a fish. The robot fish was built as part of a research project.

Alvin is launched

Alvin is a manned submersible. It also has two robot arms for manipulating scientific instruments on the seabed and collecting samples as deep as 13,124 ft (4,000 m). It sometimes carries an unmanned robot explorer called Jason Jr.

Getting a grip

Many robots have an end effector, often called a gripper, which grasps or manipulates an object in some way. Robot grippers can be built to handle a type of object with as much skill – if not more – than the human hand. Unlike robot hands, human hands can manipulate a far greater variety of objects. A human hand can pick up a grain of rice, a heavy brick, or a delicate, irregularly shaped object, with ease. By building robot hands that simulate some of the ways that the human hand works, robotics researchers are investigating how the human brain and hand work together to grip so many different objects. Once it is discovered how this is done, fully working robot equivalents may be built.

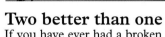

Two better than one
If you have ever had a broken arm, you quickly realize how many tasks require two hands. This pair of robot hands is designed to work closely together to pour drinks and serve food. One day, it is hoped that robot hands could serve hospital patients.

Atlas gripper
The amount of force required to grip an object is vital. Too much and an object may buckle or break. Too little and the object will not stay gripped for long. This Atlas robot hand is instructed to close around a machine part carefully to hold it without damage.

It's electric
This is one of the hand's 12 electric motors, one for each of the three joints on each digit. The motor turns to shorten or extend the tendon.

Where it's at
Optical encoders (p. 13) measure the position of each hand joint to see where it is positioned and how far it has moved.

Cybhand
Built to investigate force control, Cybhand has three fingers and a thumb with joints like a human hand. All the joints are linked via tendonlike cables to a pulley system moved by electric motors.

Just one
A cable connects Cybhand to its controller. Although its operations are highly complex, Cybhand requires only a single microprocessor to control it.

Follow the drill

Human and robot hands are both extremely versatile end effectors. Industrial robots' end effectors are often more specialized. This industrial robot's end effector is used solely for drilling and smoothing rough edges around holes in sheet metal.

Repeat learning

Cybhand's microprocessor is fed details of how much force and movement is required to hold a certain object. It learns from this so that it can repeat its actions with the same-shaped object and even adapt to new objects.

Strain gauge
Within the main link of each digit is a strain gauge, which is a sensor that estimates the amount of force being generated on the object held.

Joint
Each strain gauge is linked to a joint. The gauge measures the amount of movement and force required in the joint to grasp the object.

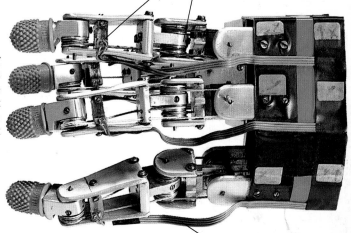

Tendons
Inside this red cable, called a sheath, is one of Cybhand's tendons that enable its joints to move.

Opening and closing
The tendons are connected to the joints of the hand. The distance that the tendon cables are pulled determines how far the fingers open and close.

Wire to microprocessor
Information from the strain gauge in the thumb is fed along this wire and stored in the microprocessor. When the hand picks up a similar object later, signals are fed back telling the thumb how to behave.

Sew-and-sews
These rubber sewing thimbles on the ends of Cybhand's digits create friction, which helps the hand grip smooth objects.

Wiring information
This wire takes signals from the strain gauges at the ends of the digits back to the motors.

The real thing
With all the joints connected by tendon cables, moving one joint has an effect on another joint, just like in a real human hand.

Thumb a lift
Cybhand's thumb is supporting the egg, allowing the three fingers above to grip the egg with less force, reducing the chances of breaking it.

Suction power
These four vacuum suction grippers work on a principle similar to that of the suction feet on Robug III (pp. 20–21).

In sheets
Vacuum suction is ideal for handling large panels of metal or fragile materials such as this sheet of glass.

Other ways of holding

The human hand and many robot hands hold objects by gripping them between fingers or getting their fingers and thumb around the object's shape. Some robots use quite different methods of holding, such as electromagnetic attraction for metal parts, or vacuum suction for large, flat materials.

Remote operation

The term "tele-operated" is used to describe robots that are remote controlled by a human operator. Many robots are tele-operated, from the RMS arm (pp. 28–29) on space shuttle flights to demonstration robots moving around an exhibition, handing out leaflets. Tele-operated robots rely on a human operator sending out commands that influence the robot's direction and speed of movement as well as its other functions. Usually, this link is two-way. The robot sends back signals showing the human controller that it has, indeed, performed what it has been asked to do. These signals are known as telemetry. A tele-operated bomb disposal robot called Hobo appears on these pages.

Disarming a bomb
The water disrupter fires an incredibly powerful blast of water into the bomb, breaking up the explosive so quickly that the igniter does not reach it until it is in small, relatively ineffectual parts.

Hobo's accessories
A bomb disposal robot, such as Hobo, shown right, can be fitted with a huge range of accessories for different tasks, including a key-turning attachment and an X-ray unit.

Finger disrupter
Disrupters come in different sizes. This is a small one.

Claw
The cat claw is used for grabbing objects.

Probe
The steel probe is often used for breaking windows.

What a star!
Star is a mine detector that can be tele-operated via a wireless data link from a safe distance away. Its two spiral tracks are hollow, giving Star enough bouyancy to travel across waterlogged ground.

Center of gravity
Hobo's low center of gravity helps it balance at steep angles.

Video display for pictures from Hobo's video camera system

Controller
Hobo's controller is manned by a human operator. It is built ruggedly for use outdoors. Hobo also comes with a portable controller, allowing the operator to move along with the robot.

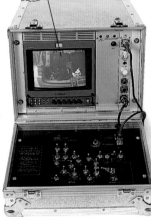

Sloping off
Hobo's six wheels and hinged body allow it to climb steps and steep ground with ease. When building the Mars rover (pp. 30–31), NASA found that their six-wheeled design could scale obstacles three times the size manageable by a four-wheeled version.

Arm camera
Close-up pictures of the end effector and its operations, recorded by this camera, enable the operator to monitor Hobo's actions.

Shotgun
Hobo can be equipped with a shotgun, which is used to gain access, for example, by shooting through a door lock.

Arm

Piston

Hydraulic oil

Piston

Wires to computer

Hydraulics
Hobo's arm is powered by hydraulics. The hydraulics system here uses one piston to compress oil in a cylinder, which in turn applies a great deal of pressure to a second piston, causing the robot arm to move.

Rear video camera
This camera provides another view of the proceedings and can be used as an aiming device for the shotgun.

Bomb disposal robot
Hobo is a tele-operated bomb disposal robot, built to withstand the detonation of a small bomb. (Its name in full is the hazardous ordnance bomb operator.) Built largely from steel and aluminum, it has a low base and good arm manipulation, making it ideal for accessing and diffusing car bombs.

A good view
The camera fitting, which has its own motor, can angle the lens in an arc of 360°.

Like the real thing
Virtual reality can give a robot's operator a better idea of the environment around the robot. Visual and tactile feedback is harnessed by advanced computers and 3D displays, such as these goggles.

Hydraulics
The arm is moved up and down by the hydraulic cylinder.

Wireless link
Hobo's radio control unit transmits to and from the operator.

The base can swing 220° in both directions

Drive camera
Hobo's third camera, at the base of the robot, is immovable.

Electrically driven
Each wheel is driven by its own electric motor and transmission. These give Hobo a top speed of 3 mph (4.8 kph).

Nanorobots

Technology is shrinking fast. Computing technology that would have filled a warehouse 30 years ago can now be squeezed onto a chip a fraction of the size of your thumbnail. The very smallest scale of engineering is called nanotechnology. A nanometer is a billionth of a meter, about the width of ten atoms. Nanotechnology may, one day, be capable of producing fully working robots to that scale, called nanorobots or nanobots. Working at an almost atomic level, nanobots could build complex items cheaply and repair clothes, equipment, and even people without being noticed. They could also be used to rid the atmosphere of pollution and to repair holes in the ozone layer.

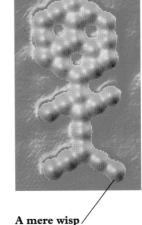

Bottom up
Researchers are looking at different ways to construct nanobots. The "bottom up" approach uses individual atoms and molecules as building blocks. This stick figure was created from just 28 carbon monoxide molecules.

A mere wisp
A row of 20,000 of these stick figures is more narrow than a human hair.

Putting it in context
A plankton skeleton, just 0.008 in (0.2 mm) across, sits on one of the engine's cogs, measuring 0.02 in (0.5 mm).

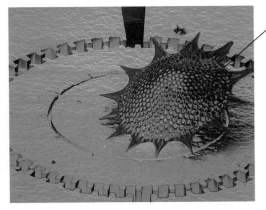

Blood vessel wall

Red blood cell

Top down
Known as "top down," one potential way of building nanomachines is to miniaturize existing machines. There have been some incredible feats, including this fully working electric motor, just 0.07 in (1.8 mm) in size.

Plaque attack
The diseased section of the blood vessel is covered with a type of plaque containing cholesterol.

Building atoms
Each ball represents one atom. The whole gear measures just a few nanometers in diameter.

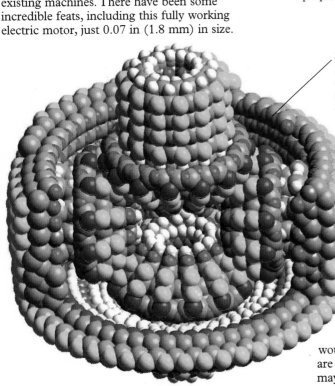

Waste away
The nanobot would either remain inside the blood system, constantly performing its task, or it would be programmed to biodegrade safely, carrying the waste plaque out of the human body.

A nanogear
Machines made from individual atoms, like this differential gear, have reached the computer modeling stage, but have not yet been built. For nanotechnology to work, they would need to be made in huge numbers. Scientists are looking to nature for ideas on how nanobots may be self-replicating, like plant and animal cells.

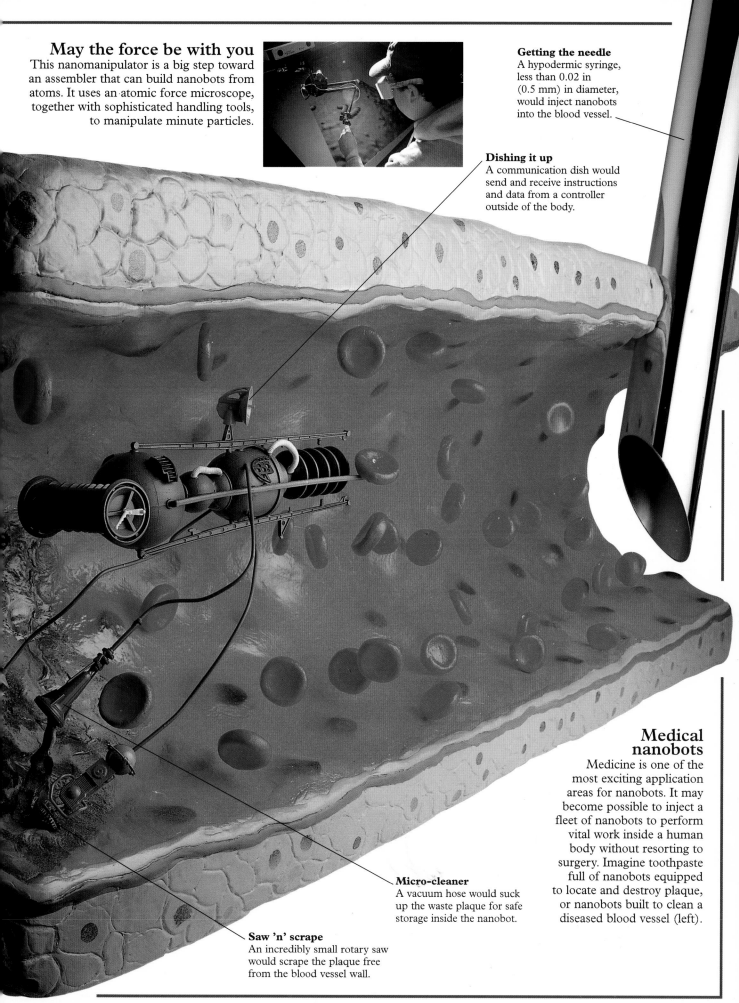

May the force be with you
This nanomanipulator is a big step toward an assembler that can build nanobots from atoms. It uses an atomic force microscope, together with sophisticated handling tools, to manipulate minute particles.

Getting the needle
A hypodermic syringe, less than 0.02 in (0.5 mm) in diameter, would inject nanobots into the blood vessel.

Dishing it up
A communication dish would send and receive instructions and data from a controller outside of the body.

Medical nanobots
Medicine is one of the most exciting application areas for nanobots. It may become possible to inject a fleet of nanobots to perform vital work inside a human body without resorting to surgery. Imagine toothpaste full of nanobots equipped to locate and destroy plaque, or nanobots built to clean a diseased blood vessel (left).

Micro-cleaner
A vacuum hose would suck up the waste plaque for safe storage inside the nanobot.

Saw 'n' scrape
An incredibly small rotary saw would scrape the plaque free from the blood vessel wall.

Robots in the near future

Fifty years ago, it was predicted that robots would be so advanced and widely used that they would be a commonplace in everyone's life. This has not happened yet and may not happen for a long time. However, robots built in research laboratories have been taught to pour drinks, pump gas, mow lawns, and perform all kinds of routine – though highly useful – chores. One day, these robots' roles will shift from the lab to the home, and they will seem as unexciting as cell phones, VCRs, and coffeemakers. Here are some concepts currently in development, including humanoid robots, robot pets, and robot communities.

Robot rover
Homes of the future may come complete with a robot pet. This robot dog is about the size of a Chihuahua. It has sensors on its "paws," and can walk, sit, and even respond to certain musical tones.

Infrared receiver
Signals are collected by the infrared receiver from any other robot in its area.

Infrared transmitter
Each robot has an infrared transmitter that sends out an individual signal of a particular frequency to other robots.

Taking the lead
This robot cannot pick up a signal from another ahead of it. It figures out that it is in front and should act as the leader.

Sending a robot ahead
The Seven Dwarfs are being used to research the possibilities of community robots. They can communicate with one another and learn. This one can sense a robot ahead.

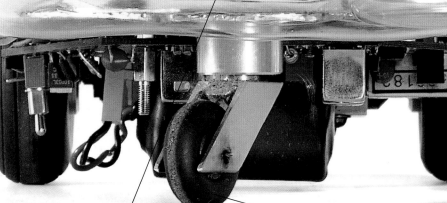

Ultrasound
Three pairs of ultrasonic transmitters and receivers are used by the robots to detect and avoid obstacles as they move.

Follow the leader
The robots are following a preprogrammed instinct to flock together – to "play" follow the leader.

Robot communities
An exciting area of research at the moment is in robot communities. These are usually collections of small robots, such as the robots above known as the Seven Dwarfs, designed to work together without human intervention. It is hoped that in the future, robot communities could, for example, search an area for unexploded bombs.

Sending signals
The lower three ultrasound sensors transmit signals. The top three receive signals.

Freewheel
There is a balancing freewheel at the front of the robot.

Avoiding each other

The two Seven Dwarf robots below are following a pre-programmed instinct to avoid each other before one decides to become the leader, as shown far left. Other courses of action have been developed as programs for the robots. These include a program called "predator," where one robot hunts down another.

Honda-Sapiens

The Honda P2 humanoid robot is nicknamed Honda-Sapiens. Our fascination with creating machines that look and act like people will continue in the future. Advances in areas of robotics research – from artificial intelligence to computer vision – are likely to be built into advanced, 21st-century humanoid robots.

Keeping balance
The P2 can walk up stairs, navigate slopes, and run. Its sophisticated internal balancing system allows it to regain its stability even if nudged or pushed.

Brain power
The robot's read-only memory (ROM) is programmed with instructions and instincts that could, for example, make the robot flock to other robots, yet avoid collisions.

Microprocessors
Messages are passed between the robot's power supply, its electronics, and its ROM by two microprocessors.

Electric connections
The robot has three layers of electric circuit boards. This cable connects the different layers.

Monitoring the robot
Lights indicate the particular instinct, of those preprogrammed in the ROM, that the robot is following at any time. They help the researchers monitor the robot's progression through the program.

Battery power
The robot knows when its battery power is low and can then search for and find a recharging station.

Round the corner
Each back wheel is powered by a separate electric motor. When one back wheel is driven and not the other, the robot turns. This allows the robot to move in very tight spaces.

Glossary

Spot-welding gun end effector

A

Actuator
A device that converts power into movement of part or all of the robot.

Analog information
Information that changes constantly. Temperature and sound are examples of analog information.

Artificial intelligence
The study of making machines do intelligent things, such as taking decisions based on information. (Experts disagree on an exact definition.)

B

Binary
Base-two number system using ones and zeroes.

Bit
A single unit of binary data used in computers.

Byte
Eight bits – a standard unit of data used by all computers.

C

Controller
The part of the robot that coordinates the robot's movement and action. It usually contains a microprocessor or a mini-computer.

D

Degrees of freedom
The term used to describe the different directions in which a robot can move. Usually, the more joints a robot has the more degrees of freedom it has.

Digital information
Information used in computers that comes in individual, separate pieces.

E

Expert system
A computer system that holds all the available information about a subject. It can be questioned by a user to provide solutions and answers.

F

Feedback
Information about the robot or its surroundings, often obtained from sensors, sent to the robot's controller.

G

Gears
Devices that increase or reduce the speed of a motor. They are found between the motor and the part that the motor is designed to drive.

Mobile research robots

Global Positioning System (GPS)
A navigation system using a series of satellites orbiting Earth to give an accurate position on Earth.

H

Hydraulics
A system using liquid (usually a form of oil) in pipes and cylinders to drive parts of a robot. Hydraulics can generate a lot of power and are used in many industrial robots.

Robot hand

I

Interface
The point at which two or more systems communicate with each other.

L

Laser
A highly focused beam of light that can be used to cut through objects and carry messages.

M

Microprocessor
The central processing unit (CPU) of a small computer. It is built onto a single wafer of silicon and can be programmed to perform a great variety of tasks.

N

Nanotechnology
The science of building machines and robots of sizes measured in nanometers. A nanometer is a billionth of a meter.

P

Payload

The maximum weight of material that a robot is capable of handling on a regular basis.

Robot submarine

AUTOSUB-1

Pitch

The up and down movement of a robot arm's wrist.

Pneumatics

A drive system that uses a gas, such as air, to power parts of a robot.

Port

The socket on a computer, into which cables joining the robot and the computer can be plugged.

Programmable

A term used to describe a robot or machine that can be given new instructions to perform new tasks.

Proximity sensing

A device that detects the presence or absence of an object within a certain distance.

R

RAM

Random-access memory. A computer's circuits that process and temporarily hold information.

Roll

The circular movement of a robot arm's wrist joint.

ROM

Read-only memory. The permanent store of programs inside a computer.

S

Servo

A small motor that drives an individual part of a robot.

Sensor

A device that gives a computer information about the robot or about the environment it is in.

Service robot

A term used to describe all working robots outside of factories.

T

Tactile sensor

A device that uses touch to provide information about an object.

Teach pendant

A handheld device that is used to record movements into the robot's memory.

Telerobot

A robot that is partially or completely controlled by a human operator via a remote link.

Transducer

A device that converts one type of energy, such as heat, light, or pressure, into electrical energy. There are many different types of transducers.

Security robot

U

Ultrasound sensing

A system of sensing that uses very high-frequency sounds, outside of the range of human hearing.

V

Voice recognition

Technology in which a robot is programmed to respond to the voice of a human operator.

W

Working envelope

The area of space that a robot's end effector can reach. It is sometimes also known as the work volume.

Y

Yaw

Side-to-side movement of a robot arm's wrist joint.

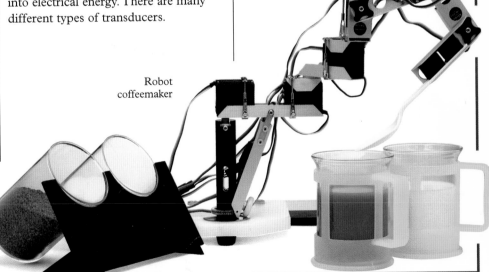

Robot coffeemaker

Index

ABC

accumulator 22
acoustic doppler current profiler (ADCP) 32
actuator 10
advanced unmanned search system (AUSS) 32
AERCam Sprint 28–29
Alvin 33
antenna 17, 23, 27, 31
arm, robot 12 13
    bomb disposal robot 36–37
    industrial 9, 14–15
    space 29, 30
    surgical 24–25
    underwater 33
armored patrol robot 8
artificial intelligence (AI) 16 17, 20, 41
assembly line 12, 14
attitude sensor 33
automata 8
automated guided vehicle (AGV) 18–19
automation 14
autonomous underwater vehicle (AUV) 32–33
autostop 18
Autosub 32–33
battery 8, 18, 23, 29, 33, 41
biped 20
bomb detector 40
bomb disposal 36–37
"bottom up" 38
bumper 18, 24
cable 10, 13, 14, 15, 22, 25, 34, 41
camera 17, 21, 22, 28–31, 37
    space 28–29
catapult 11
cat's claw 36
center of gravity 19, 36
chess 17
coffeemaker 10–11
collision avoidance 16–17, 23, 41
community robots 40–41
compressed air 21, 23
computer control 8, 10–11
conductivity instrument 32
controller 8, 10, 11, 33, 36
    stand-alone 15
cooperation 17, 40
crawler, three-legged 10
Cybhand 34–35

DEF

degrees of freedom 12, 26, 28
direct teaching 15
disrupter 36
dog, robot 40
drive system 8
electric motor 8, 12, 23, 29, 31, 34, 37, 41
    nanotechnology 38
electromagnetism 19, 35
end effector 8, 11, 12, 13, 15, 34, 35
explorer:
    Martian 31
    underwater 33
factory, see industrial robots
farm robots 26–27
feedback 8, 13, 15, 35, 37
first robot 12
fish, robot 33
flight telerobotic servicer (FTS) 29
force sensor 25
forklift AGV 18–19
freewheel 40

GHI

gear, differential 38
Geiger counter 21
glide wheel 10
global positioning system (GPS) 33
goggles, virtual reality 37
golf bag carrier 8
gripper 8, 13, 16, 17, 34
guide coil 19
guide dog, robot 22
gun 22, 23, 37
hand, robot 9, 34–35
hip replacement 24–25
Hobo 36–37
hospitals 18, 24–25, 34
humanoids 9, 41
hydraulics 9, 12, 27, 37
IBM Deep Blue 17
incremental encoder 13
industrial robots 35
    AGV 18–19
    arm 8–9, 14–15
infrared 18, 19, 22, 40
InteleCady 8

JKL

joint 11, 12, 13, 21, 35
kits 8, 10–11
Lama 31
learning 16, 35, 40
legged robot 20–21
light scanner 13

MNO

map, digital 8, 24
Mars rover 30–31, 36
maze, micro 16
medical robots 24–25
    nanobots 38–39
microprocessor 10, 20, 34, 41
milker 26
mine detector 36
miniaturization 38
motion detector 22, 25, 30
mouse 16
nanomanipulator 39
nanobot 38–39
NASA 28, 29, 30
navigation system 18
nitrogen fuel 29
nuclear industry 21
optical encoder 34
orderly, robot 24

PR

packing 14
paint spraying 14, 15
Pathfinder lander 30, 31
pet 40
pH probe 33
photoelectric cell 13
pinger 16, 17
Pioneer 1 16–17
pivot arm 27
pneumatics 12, 14, 21, 22
positional feedback 15
probe 36
    space probe 30–31
processing unit 15
programming:
    off-line 14
    walk-through 15
proximity sensor 22
radio signal 23, 29, 30, 31, 33, 37
read-only memory (ROM) 41
RCX controller 11
redundant joint 21
regulator 29
remote control, see tele-operated robot
remote manipulation system 29, 36
repeat actions 11, 13, 35
research robot 9, 12, 16, 40
Robart III 22–23
Robodoc 24–25
Robug III 20–21
rocker 31
rotor 12
route planner 8, 24
rover, planetary 30–31

ST

satellite beacon 32
science fiction 9, 17
scientific instruments 30, 32
security robot 22–23
sensors 8, 16, 18, 19, 21, 22, 23, 26, 27
servo 10, 11, 15, 27
servo controller 15
Seven Dwarfs 40–41
sheep-shearer 26–27
silicon chip 10, 38
simulation 13
soccer competition 16–17
Sojourner 30–31
solar panel 31
sonar 16, 17, 27, 32
space 28–31
space camera 28–29
space shuttle 28, 29
space station 29
spacewalk 29
spot welding 14–15
Sprint camera, see AERCam Sprint
stator coils 12
steering 23
strain gauge 35
submersible 32–33
supermarket trolley 18
surgical robot 24–25
telemetry 36
tele-operated robot 32, 36–37
tendon 35
thruster 28, 29
"top down" 38

UV

ultrasound 18, 23, 27, 40
underwater robots 32–33
Unimate 12
vacuum suction 20, 35
vehicle, see automated guided vehicle
video camera, see camera
Viking 1 probe 30
virtual reality 24, 37
vision 9, 16, 17, 22–23, 41
walking gait 21
wheels 8, 23, 30, 31, 36, 41
wire guidance system 19
wool 26
work station 11, 24
working envelope 18

Acknowledgements

The publisher would like to thank:
Professor Kevin Warwick, Michael Hilton, Darren Wenn, and Dr. David Keating of the Department of Cybernetics, University of Reading, UK (pp. 20–21, 34–35, and 40–41); particularly Professor Kevin Warwick for acting as consultant for pp. 10–11, 16–17, 20–21, 34–35, 38–39, and 40–41; Peter Rowe and Dave Pearson of Kawasaki Robotics Ltd (pp. 8–9 and 12–15); Dr. Bing L. Luk of the Department of Electrical and Electronic Engineering, University of Portsmouth, UK and Theo K Kalyvas of Portech (pp. 20–21); the Natural Environment Research Council who funded Autosub and Nick Millard of the Southampton Oceanography Centre, UK (pp. 32–33); Kate Howey and Elgan Loane of Kentree Ltd,

Ireland (pp. 36–37); Lynn Miller and Gary Conrad (pp. 8–9); Evan Rosen and Advanced Design, Inc. (www.robix.com) for the use of their Robix ™ RCS-6 construction set (pp. 10–11); Barry Werger and Jeanne Dietsch (pp. 16–17); AGV Products, Inc. (pp. 18–19); Bart Everett of SPAWAR Systems Center (pp. 22–23); Integrated Surgical Systems, Inc. and Professor Brian Davies (pp. 24–25); Professor James Trevelyan and the Shear Magic team of the Department of Mechanical and Materials Engineering, University of Western Australia (pp. 26–27); Roy Margolis.

Artwork: Carlton Hibbert

Additional photography: Andy Crawford and Dave King; assistance

from Gary Ombler and Kim Watson

Design assistance: Darren Troughton, Catherine Goldsmith, Venice Shone, and Maggie Tingle

Index: Chris Bernstein

Picture Credits:
Key: t=top; b=below; c= center; l=left; r=right

Art Directors & TRIP Photo Library: NASA 30tr, Associated Press 40tl, Barnaby's Picture Library: Antonia Reeve 26tr, Ford Motor Company 12tr, Helpmate Robotics 24cl, IBM 17tr & 38tr, IMM 38bl, Kawasaki Robots 15br, Kobal Collection 9tl & 17ca, NASA 28tr, cl,c, bl, 29cl, cl, br, 33br, NCCOSC 22t, b (all),

Rex Features 16br, Right Image/Comau UK Ltd 15tr, Robodoc 24cr, Science & Society Picture Library 30-1b, Science Photo Library: Julian Balm 41tr, Marcello Bertinetti 9cl, P Dumas/Eurelios 31tl, Davidier, Jerrican 18tr, Bruce Frisch 29tr, Jerrican 18tr, George Haling 14bl, Adam Hart-Davis 8cl, M Hulyk 24bl, Manfred Kage 38cl, Lawrence Livermore/National Laboratory 36cb, Dick Luria 37tl, Jerry Mason 36cl, Peter Menzel 37clb, Hank Morgan 21bl, 24tr, 25bl, NASA 31bl, Sam Ogden 9bl & 32bl, Rosenfeld Images Ltd 18bl, Tadandri Salfo 36tr, Geoff Tompinson 10tr, Stan Wayman 32br, Peter Yates 22cr, Silsoe Research Institute 26 bl, University of Southampton 32tr.